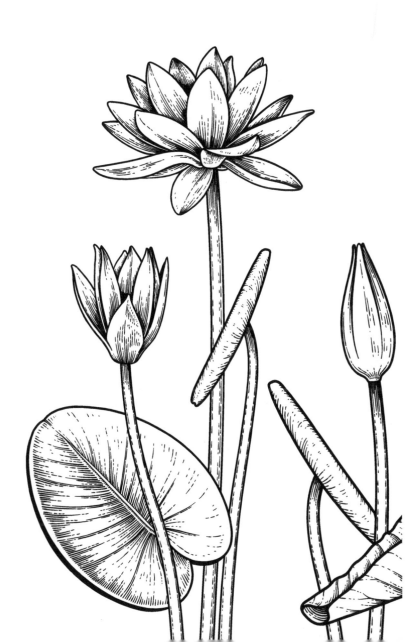

Original Title: Infinite Horizon

Editors: Theodor Taimla
Autor: Marlen Vesiroos
ISBN 978-9916-748-85-5

Infinite Horizon

Marlen Vesiroos

Ever-lasting Roads

Upon the paths where shadows blend,
Where dawn and dusk eternally bend,
We tread through dreams with hearts so vast,
On ever-lasting roads we've cast.

With each step, the echoes grow,
Their whispers serenade our woe,
In twilight's arms, we find our rest,
On journeys where our souls are blessed.

The stars above, our guiding lights,
Through endless days and boundless nights,
We weave through time, where hope unfolds,
On ever-lasting roads untold.

Journey's End and Beyond

At the threshold where echoes hum,
We breathe as one, our song begun,
The end is near, yet far it streams,
A journey's end within our dreams.

Through valleys broad where shadows creep,
We find the promises we keep,
The path ahead may twist and wind,
But in our hearts, the light we'll find.

With every footfall, every stride,
We glimpse the stars that never hide,
And though we part, our spirits blend,
On journeys that will never end.

Onward to Always

Through fields of gold and cliffs so sheer,
We march with will, with hearts sincere,
The road is long, our vision clear,
Onward to always, without fear.

The sky that looms, an endless dome,
Beneath it, we, forever roam,
With courage rich and spirits high,
We chase the limits of the sky.

Beyond the hills where sun meets sea,
We carve a path for all to see,
With every dawn, a fresh embrace,
Onward to always, in endless grace.

To the Boundless Unknown

Into the night where whispers call,
We venture forth, embracing all,
The unknown trails, a siren's hymn,
From edge of known to star's own rim.

Beneath the vast, uncharted skies,
Where mystery and wonder rise,
We weave our tales in cosmic thread,
Through realms where fears and dreams are wed.

With every pulse, the voids ignite,
With dreams that pierce the dark of night,
And though we sail through endless space,
To the boundless unknown, we race.

Timeless Expanse

In a world where time stands still,
Whispers of the past remain.
Stars above with silent grace,
Mark the centuries' refrain.

Shadows dance on ancient stones,
Stories told in muted hue.
History in winds that blow,
A canvas painted blue.

Mountains tall where echoes hide,
Secrets of a thousand years.
River's song that carves the land,
Gently soothes forgotten fears.

Eternal Frontier

Where the edge of dreams resides,
Boundaries dissolve and fade.
Horizons stretch to realms unseen,
Amid the twilight's cascade.

Beyond the known, the heart leaps bold,
Seeks the undiscovered path.
Mysteries wrapped in twilight's glow,
Awaiting daring swath.

Voices call from distant shores,
Brimming with celestial lore.
Journey forth with open heart,
To find what lies in store.

Beyond the Brink

On the verge of endless night,
Stars converge and softly sing.
Guiding through the void unknown,
To dreams on stardust wing.

Venturing where light fades thin,
Yet hope remains a guiding spark.
Bound to neither earth nor time,
We navigate the dark.

Echoes from the void resound,
Spirits of the brave and free.
Charting courses through the realms,
Where destiny must be.

Vast Beyond

In the vast beyond we sail,
Undertow of cosmic seas.
Galaxies like diamonds strewn,
Among celestial trees.

Wanderers we've always been,
Questing through the velvet night.
Steered by winds of ancient stars,
Seeking out the light.

Tales of old and futures new,
Interweave in endless dance.
Eyes alight with boundless hope,
We journey through the expanse.

Endless Twilight

In the glow of fading light,
Shadows dance in soft embrace.
Whispers of the coming night,
Hold the sky in velvet grace.

Stars ignite, the dusk unfolds,
Veil of dreams begins to rise.
Mysteries the darkness holds,
Woven in the twilight skies.

Silent symphony of stars,
Paints the heavens' vast domain.
Where the night its peace imparts,
In the twilight's tender reign.

The Boundless Edge

At the edge of dreams we stand,
Gazing past the known terrains.
Endless waves of untamed lands,
Stretch beyond the mind's remains.

Horizons fade to purple hues,
Where the earth and sky converge.
In this realm, our thoughts diffuse,
Into whispers on the verge.

Endless possibilities,
Call us from the boundless brink.
Where the stars and destinies,
Float like feathers on the ink.

Everlasting Distance

Between the echoes of our hearts,
Lies an ocean deep and wide.
Waves of time that drift apart,
In their ceaseless, transient tide.

Across the miles, our thoughts align,
In the silence of the night.
Messages like stars that shine,
Bind our spirits in their light.

Through the distance, ever vast,
Dreams and wishes intertwine.
Memories from future's past,
Link our souls in endless line.

Uncharted Skies

In the realms of boundless blue,
Wings of hope take flight anew.
Where the sun and dreams pursue,
Secrets of the skies break through.

Clouds like whispers gently soar,
Marking paths not walked before.
Every sight a new explore,
In the skies that hold yet more.

Stars above in silent aire,
Guide the way through night's affair.
Charting dreams beyond compare,
In the skies without despair.

Both Ends of Forever

In the quiet hush of twilight's grace,
We dance on edges of time's embrace.
From first soft light to evening's close,
In love's eternal, gentle repose.

We weave our dreams in starry threads,
Across the skies above our heads.
Through days and nights, our spirits blend,
At both ends of forever, without end.

With every breath, a whispered vow,
To cherish, here and now.
In endless time, our hearts entwine,
Both ends of forever, yours and mine.

Endless Dawn

The night gives way to morning's glow,
A brighter path for us to know.
In golden beams of rising sun,
A new beginning has begun.

Through valleys deep and mountains high,
We chase the light that paints the sky.
Each dawn a promise, fresh and clear,
Endless hope and absence of fear.

Together we will face the day,
With love to guide us on our way.
In endless dawn, we find our might,
To overcome the darkest night.

The Vanishing Line

On the edge where worlds collide,
A vanishing line where dreams reside.
Between the known and the unseen,
A whisper of what might have been.

Through mist and shadow, glimpses fade,
Of hopes and fears the twilight made.
Invisible, yet felt so true,
The line that hides between the view.

Where reality and dream align,
We search to trace the vanishing line.
In the twilight's silver haze,
Caught between the light and shade.

Beyond the Blue

In skies that stretch to endless heights,
We soar beyond the blue-lit nights.
Through constellations' glittering dance,
We find our way in vast expanse.

Beyond the realms of earthly bind,
In cosmic wonders, we unwind.
A journey set by stars and moon,
In silence of the night's soft tune.

With dreams alight in radiant hue,
We chase the mysteries, old yet new.
Forever seeking, hearts so true,
Our destiny beyond the blue.

Endless Pursuit

In shadows deep, we seek our light,
Through winding paths, both day and night.
With hearts ablaze, we chase our dream,
A ceaseless quest, a flowing stream.

We climb the hills, and cross the plains,
With every step, the goal remains.
Through trials vast, and joys we find,
This endless pursuit defines our mind.

Beneath the stars, our spirits soar,
Yearning always to explore.
A dance of hopes, a journey grand,
Together moving hand in hand.

Across the Expanse

Gazing out to distant lands,
Where horizon meets the sands.
A journey starts with hopes anew,
Under skies of azure blue.

Mountains high and rivers wide,
Nature's grandeur at our side.
Steps we take with courage strong,
Hearts alive, a hopeful song.

From dawn till dusk, in twilight hues,
Every mile, a story true.
The world unfolds its wondrous dance,
As we travel, lost in trance.

Eternal Offering

In every bloom, a tale is spun,
Of moments passed and days begun.
A gift of life in colors bright,
Eternal offering to the night.

Whispered winds through leaves do sing,
A serenade to herald spring.
Nature's bounty, freely shared,
In every fragrance, love is bared.

The sun and moon, in endless tune,
Their gentle light, a soft cocoon.
With every dawn, the world renews,
In boundless ways, it pays its dues.

Sky Without Limits

Look above, the sky's expanse,
A realm where dreams and hopes can dance.
No borders drawn, no chains to bind,
An endless canvas for the mind.

Clouds that drift and stars that gleam,
A universe where spirits dream.
Wings of thought take boundless flight,
In this vast, unending night.

Horizons blend, horizons part,
With every gaze, we find new art.
A sky without limits, free and grand,
An infinite realm, at our command.

Over the Threshold

With steps of hope, we cross the line,
Into realms we've yet to find.
Whispers of futures, soft and fine,
Chase the shadows from the mind.

Worlds of light, beyond the door,
Where dreams take flight, and spirits soar.
The echoes of our past implore,
But forward, onward we explore.

Through twilight's veil, where stars amend,
New tales ready to ascend.
Hand in hand, good souls befriend,
On paths unknown, to journey's end.

Beyond the Pale

Where twilight meets the whispering night,
And shadows dance in silvered light.
Beyond the pale, where dreams ignite,
We find our truth, in endless flight.

In lands where daylight never dies,
The stars become our lullabies.
Through vast expanse, with open eyes,
We chase the dawn across the skies.

Against the dark, our hearts will sail,
Past borders old, a hopeful trail.
Embrace the world, beyond the pale,
In lands of light, where love prevails.

Endless Passage

In corridors of time we roam,
With memories, our hearts are home.
An endless passage, yet unknown,
With every step, new seeds are sewn.

The hourglass, its sands now stream,
Through nights of wonder, days agleam.
Within our hearts, the whispers teem,
Of paths unseen, and endless dream.

In twilight's glow, where silence sings,
To hidden realms, the passage springs.
As time unfurls, the essence clings,
To timeless truths, that journey brings.

Unyielding Horizon

Where earth meets sky, a line unseen,
The unyielding horizon keen.
With every breath, and thought serene,
We chase the edge, where worlds convene.

The sun and moon, they light our way,
Through night and day, an endless play.
In search of dreams that never stay,
Yet guide us forth, come what may.

With courage bold, and hearts upright,
We sail to distant lands of light.
No storm nor shadow can incite,
A pause in our unyielding flight.

Unfathomable Reach

In the depths where shadows play,
Chasing dreams both night and day,
Silent whispers, untold lore,
Mysteries linger evermore.

Waves that crash on silent shores,
Echoes of forgotten wars,
Stars above in patterns strange,
Guiding paths through realms of change.

Beneath the surface, stories lie,
Abyssal realms where spirits fly,
Tales of old in waters deep,
Secrets lost in endless sleep.

Diving down, the heart must brace,
Facing truths in hidden space,
Worlds within where none may breach,
Stretching to unfathomable reach.

Perpetual Vista

Horizon meets the dreaming eyes,
Boundless as the open skies,
Mountains rise where eagles soar,
Nature's canvas, evermore.

Valleys lush in emerald green,
Mystic rivers' silver sheen,
Whispers of the ancient trees,
Carry tales upon the breeze.

Sunset's blaze, a burning art,
Reflecting fire, a beating heart,
Twilight's hues, so softly blend,
Day to night in hues ascend.

Infinite, the world unbounded,
By beauty's touch, we're astounded,
Eternal scenes both near and far,
In the sky's perpetual vista.

Ceaseless Journey

Step by step, we tread the path,
Facing storms with gentle wrath,
Eyes fixed ever on the prize,
Under boundless, changing skies.

Winding roads with secrets bare,
Every turn and twist we dare,
Mountains loom and valleys low,
Onward still we boldly go.

Through the night and through the day,
Finding peace in disarray,
Maps that guide or lead astray,
Wanderlust will find its way.

Paths no end, horizons wide,
With the stars our trust and guide,
Undeterred by fate's decree,
On this ceaseless journey, free.

Unending Blue

Sky above in vast expanse,
Ocean's waves in endless dance,
Azure realms both deep and true,
Unfold the tale of unending blue.

Wandering clouds and tides that sway,
Mirroring night, reflecting day,
Boundless depths and heavens high,
Mingle where horizons lie.

Birds that sail on winds aflight,
Sailors' dreams in starlit night,
Whales that sing their ancient song,
In these depths, we all belong.

Eyes that gaze to one embrace,
Void of time and empty space,
Hearts aloft in tranquil view,
Ever lost in unending blue.

Limitless Landscape

Horizon stretches far and wide,
Where earth and sky converge.
A boundless, open countryside,
In nature we submerge.

The mountains whisper ancient tales,
As rivers thread the seam.
In valleys where the heart prevails,
We wander in a dream.

The endless field of golden grain,
Bows humbly to the breeze.
In this expanse, we break our chains,
And find our spirits eased.

Perpetual Light

A glimmer pierces through the veil,
Of dark and endless night.
An ember's spark, a guiding trail,
That fills the heart with might.

Through shadowed paths, it softly gleams,
To lead us from despair.
A canvas for our wildest dreams,
With hope beyond compare.

Across the stars, its rays extend,
A dance of radiant grace.
In perpetual light, we mend,
Dispel our fears, embrace.

Vast and Boundless

The sky above, so vast and boundless,
A tapestry of blue.
Within its depths, a world so soundless,
Where we are ever true.

The ocean swells with boundless might,
Its waves forever grand.
A symphony of day and night,
That meets the endless land.

With each horizon, we are shown,
A life without restriction.
In spaces vast, our spirits flown,
Beyond all life's affliction.

The Great Beyond

Where morning light meets twilight's end,
A realm of endless skies.
The heavens beckon, stars extend,
Their silent, watchful eyes.

The galaxies afar, they gleam,
In cosmic symmetry.
In dreams we touch their woven seam,
Immersed in mystery.

In this expanse, what lies ahead,
No mortal eyes have seen.
A path where all our fears are shed,
To worlds serene and green.

Eternal Escapade

In lands where whispers hold the night,
We chase the dreams of morning light.
Through shadows dense and valleys wide,
Our spirits soar, with stars our guide.

The moonlight dances on the sea,
A symphony of mystery.
We sail on waves of destiny,
To realms where hearts forever flee.

Each step we take, a timeless stride,
In search of wonders, far and wide.
Boundless skies and endless glades,
Our journey's path, an escapade.

The mountains call, the rivers sing,
In nature's arms, we find our spring.
With every breath, a new parade,
In this eternal escapade.

The Depthless Beyond

Beyond the veil of twilight's hue,
A boundless realm of endless blue.
Where stars ignite in cosmic play,
Whispering secrets of the day.

In nebulae, our dreams entwine,
With galaxies our fates align.
The universe, a silent song,
Invites our souls to come along.

Through blackened space and time's delight,
We wander in the endless night.
Our hearts, they beat in astral rhyme,
Exploring eons, lost in time.

Eternal vistas, pure and grand,
Unfold beneath our wandering hand.
In this depthless, vast expanse,
We find the courage for our dance.

Unending Odyssey

Across the plains, through desert's heat,
Our journey is a feat so sweet.
The wanderer's heart, it knows no home,
To distant lands, it yearns to roam.

Through forests dense and rivers wide,
With nature as our faithful guide.
Each step we take, a tale begun,
Underneath the golden sun.

The night unfolds, the stars awake,
In silence, dreams begin to quake.
The odyssey, it never ends,
With every dawn, a path ascends.

Mountains rise, yet we ascend,
In every curve, our spirits bend.
An odyssey, forever flows,
In every heart, the journey grows.

Timeless Trail

In ancient woods where secrets lie,
The whispers of the past imply,
A trail that winds through history,
Where time and space entwine the free.

The river's song, the winds embrace,
A silent dance, a gentle chase.
We tread the path of ageless lore,
To find what came and what's in store.

Each leaf, a tale, each branch, a guide,
Through memories, our spirits glide.
The footsteps echo, loud and clear,
On trails untamed, we venture near.

The horizon fades, yet still we quest,
For in the journey lies our rest.
A timeless trail where dreams prevail,
And in its endlessness, we sail.

Whispers of Eternity

In the stillness of the night,
Whispers travel through the air.
Softly singing ancient tales,
Of love and dreams laid bare.

Stars above, as silent guides,
Impart secrets, old and wise.
Time itself a fleeting blur,
Within our brief yet endless skies.

Each moment like a fragile note,
One in a symphony of light.
Eternity's a whispered breath,
In the silence of the night.

Edge of the World

Where the oceans meet the sky,
Stand we at the edge unfurled.
Mountains tall as thoughts profound,
Gazing on the endless world.

Windswept strands of golden sand,
Footprints mark our transient stay.
Seagulls cry and soar above,
Tracing dreams that slip away.

Here at nature's grand divide,
Boundaries of hope and fear.
We discover in the vast,
We're both nowhere, and we're here.

Stretching to Infinity

Through the fields of time we roam,
Stretching out to touch the stars.
Every moment stretched and grown,
Binds our hearts in unseen bars.

Infinitesimal our stride,
Yet grand dreams within us bloom.
Reach beyond the farthest tide,
Let not shadows weave our doom.

In the dance of cosmic hues,
Hand in hand, two souls align.
In the vast, we find our truth,
Stretching to infinity's sign.

Chasing the Unseen

Across the meadows of our dreams,
We wander paths that time forgot.
Seeking out the hidden seams,
Where the seen and unseen knot.

Catching whispers in the breeze,
Shadows dance in moonlit glow.
With each step, our hearts appease,
Mysteries we yearn to know.

Through the veil of twilight hues,
Guided by the stars above.
In pursuit of all things true,
Chasing the unseen we love.

Boundless Timelessness

In the stillness, time unfolds the veil,
Moments lingering, soft whispers sail.
Endless echoes, beyond space they weave,
In eternity's grasp, we believe.

Stars and shadows, dance without cease,
Eternal twilight, a silent peace.
Dreams float gently on the cosmic tide,
In boundless timelessness, we confide.

Seasons come and blurry go,
Hours meld in a seamless flow.
Time, unbroken, a river profound,
Where beginnings nor ends are found.

Infinite Trek

On paths unseen, our steps proceed,
To quests unknown where secrets lead.
Footfalls echo in silent lands,
Guided softly by unseen hands.

Mountains, valleys, stretch afar,
Underneath a watchful star.
Horizons call where sky meets sea,
In this infinite trek, we are free.

Winds may whisper, leaves may sigh,
Through forests old, beneath the sky.
Every journey starts with a spark,
In the trek of the infinite dark.

The Never-Ending Veil

Veils of twilight gently drift,
Shadows weave a secret gift.
Luminous threads in night's embrace,
Weaving tales that time won't erase.

Deep within the midnight blue,
Mysteries linger, wondrous and true.
Underneath the silent moon,
In the never-ending veil's tune.

Stars like diamonds, skies adorned,
Ancient whispers, souls reborn.
Through the veil, we glimpse the past,
In the endless night, shadows cast.

Boundless Skies

Eyes cast upward, dreams take flight,
Stars illuminate the endless night.
Clouds like whispers, softly roam,
In boundless skies, we find our home.

Wings unfurl to touch the sun,
In celestial fields, our race begun.
Beyond the horizon, far and wide,
In these skies, our spirits glide.

Azure depths, bright and vast,
Where future and past are cast.
Boundless skies, with whispers strewn,
Guiding us through night and noon.

Beyond the Ends of Time

In the quiet, whispered hush,
Where stars align in nightly rush,
Beyond where dreams and darkness climb,
Lies the end, beyond the time.

Echoes of a life once lived,
Through spaces, moments gently sieved,
In the void where shadows chime,
We wander past the ends of time.

Silver threads of cosmic lace,
Bind the past in their embrace,
Infinite, the ghostly rhyme,
Guiding us beyond the time.

Dimensional Leap

Stepping through the veil unseen,
To realms where the impossible's been,
A shadow slips, a secret keap,
Into the void, a dimensional leap.

Lights that dance on unseen threads,
Whisper softly to the dead,
In this space, where silence keeps,
The secrets of the stars that weep.

Every moment, shifting fast,
Future, present, meld with past,
Through the vast, the unknown deep,
We journey on a dimensional leap.

Endless Beyond

Gaze into the sapphire skies,
Where countless, timeless echoes lie,
Beyond the edge, to realms unknown,
Exists a place where souls are grown.

In the space between the stars,
Silent whispers tell of scars,
That bind the light, yet travel on,
Through the endless, boundless beyond.

Shadows dance in twilight's gleam,
Reality, but just a dream,
In the depths where souls are drawn,
We find the endless, timeless beyond.

The Everlasting Trace

In the stillness of the night,
Where the moon provides its light,
Lingers there, a sacred place,
Etched with time, the everlasting trace.

Silent winds that softly blow,
Carry tales from long ago,
In their wake, the signs they place,
Marking paths, the everlasting trace.

Through the ages, ancient lore,
Echoes from a distant shore,
In each heart, the timeless lace,
Weave the ever, lasting trace.

The Eternal Blur

In the twilight, shadows twist and turn,
Whispering secrets only night can earn.
Dreams entwine with reality's blur,
In that moment, worlds are interred.

Midnight winds carry echoes past,
Where memories of time will last.
Stars fade as dawn breaks near,
Yet fragments of night never clear.

Ethereal mists cloak the ground,
In silence, the lost are found.
Boundaries of light and dark unfurl,
In the eternal blur, we swirl.

Eyes closed in waking dreams,
Where the ephemeral softly gleams.
A dance between the realms occur
In the endless, eternal blur.

Time bends in twilight's embrace,
Moments blend, no need to chase.
Caught in a world both here and there,
In the eternal blur, we share.

Beyond the Veil

Whispers float on the evening air,
Of tales and dreams left to spare.
Curtains of dusk, so thin and frail,
Reveal the path beyond the veil.

Shadows dance in ghostly light,
Guiding us through endless night.
Mysteries of stars in silence trail,
Leading us beyond the veil.

In silence we find hidden keys,
Unlocking truths like ancient seas.
Time distorts, old echoes wail,
Calling us beyond the veil.

Glimpses of the past and future reign,
In the space where none can feign.
Within this realm, no heart can fail,
It beckons all beyond the veil.

Pilgrims of night, seekers of dawn,
We walk through dreams, from dusk till yawn.
In darkened times, our hopes unveil,
A journey endless, beyond the veil.

The Limitless Edge

Standing where the earth meets sky,
We watch as the limits defy.
Horizons stretch, endlessly wide,
At the limitless edge, dreams reside.

Waves crash and recede in turn,
Endless cycles where fires burn.
Each step forward, unknown stride,
Into the limitless edge, we slide.

Stars above, like beacons bright,
Guide us through the endless night.
On this cusp, the worlds collide,
Chasing the limitless edge with pride.

In the silence of the boundless blue,
Reflections of me and you.
Echoes whisper, none can hide,
On the limitless edge, side by side.

With courage as our guiding light,
We'll soar into the endless height.
Every moment, new and tried,
We embrace the limitless edge, open and wide.

Timeless Boundaries

In realms where time does not bind,
We traverse the corridors of mind.
Eternal visions, clear and sound,
Within these timeless boundaries found.

Whispers of the ancient past,
In moments that forever last.
Futures merge, the present crowned,
Marking timeless boundaries unbound.

In the stillness, worlds unfold,
Lilting through the tales untold.
Chronicles in silence surround,
Echoing in timeless boundaries profound.

Across the ages, voices sing,
Every note and echoing ring.
In the realm where sights astound,
Lie the timeless boundaries around.

From dawn to dusk, and night to day,
In this place, we find our way.
Endless line where love is found,
Holding to timeless boundaries, sound.

Skyward Bound

Horizons paint the morning fair,
With hues of gold in sunlit air,
The azure sky, so vast and wide,
Calls forth the hearts that dare to glide.

Beyond the clouds where dreams take flight,
A world unfolds in purest light,
Where eagles soar and stars confide,
In whispers of the night sky wide.

Each breath of wind, a song so sweet,
Lifts tired souls from earthly seat,
To realms where gravity holds no sway,
And skyward bounds the spirits play.

Sunsets blend with twilight's song,
Inviting those who long belong,
To journey where the heavens meet,
And find the sky beneath their feet.

For in the blue, our hopes are crowned,
In endless skies, our hearts unbound,
We chase the clouds and stars profound,
Forevermore, we're skyward bound.

Unseen Paths

Through forests dense and valleys deep,
Where shadows dance and secrets keep,
Unseen paths begin to wind,
Calling to the curious mind.

Steps that tread on whispering leaves,
Unfold the tales that nature weaves,
Each footfall writes a story new,
On paths that hide from common view.

Mysteries in moonlit haze,
Guide us through the earthly maze,
Where silence speaks and echoes find,
The melody of paths aligned.

With each new turn, the unknown calls,
Through whispered woods and secret halls,
In every tree and silent glen,
Unseen paths await again.

So venture forth with open eyes,
To where the hidden beauty lies,
For in these trails, both small and grand,
Lie unseen paths by nature's hand.

Endless Frontier

Where land meets sky in endless reach,
A frontier vast beyond our speech,
Mountains rise, with peaks so clear,
To touch the edge, the frontier near.

The whispering winds, the calling seas,
Invite us to their mysteries,
A boundless stretch, a wild expanse,
Where dreams and reality dance.

Through deserts dry and rivers wide,
We chart our course, our fate decides,
In quest of sights we've never seen,
To landscapes vast, both bold and keen.

Horizons melt with twilight hues,
In colors bold, purples, blues,
The frontier's call, so loud and pure,
Beckons hearts to venture sure.

Beyond the known, beyond the here,
Lie endless realms, the frontier dear,
To mark our paths in history's ear,
And chase the dreams frontiers endear.

The Great Expanse

Beneath the stars, a canvas wide,
Where dreams and endless hopes abide,
The great expanse, in silence speaks,
In waves of light and cosmic peaks.

Each star a story, burning bright,
In tapestry of endless night,
Beyond our grasp, yet close at hand,
The universe, a wonderland.

Planets spin in cosmic dance,
In rhythm of the vast expanse,
Galaxies swirl in endless flight,
A celestial ballet in the night.

Nebulas, in colors stream,
Crafting visions, like a dream,
In every hue, life forms commune,
Beneath the silver, glowing moon.

For in this great, unmeasured space,
We find our place, a tiny trace,
A part of something grand and true,
The great expanse, both old and new.

The Forever Line

On endless paths our souls entwine,
Through twilight's glow, in dusk's design.
Whispers of dreams, our hearts align,
In shadows deep, the forever line.

As stars emerge, the night begins,
With every step, our love thickens.
Silent echoes where light thins,
A journey onward, our hearts akin.

Moonlight dances on a silver stream,
Guiding us within this dream.
Eternal tides, a gentle gleam,
Together forever, or so it seems.

Boundless time, our sacred vow,
Through endless fields, we plow;
Hand in hand, we take a bow,
In eternity's glow, here and now.

Voices soften, moments align,
In soft embrace, we find our shrine.
Through the ages, spirits combine,
In the soft touch, the forever line.

The Celestial Journey

Beyond the sky, where stars ignite,
We chase the shadows of the night.
In cosmic winds, our souls take flight,
A celestial journey, pure delight.

Through nebula fields of colored hue,
Our spirits rise, renewed and true.
Infinity's canvas, vast and blue,
A voyage shared by me and you.

Galaxies spin in endless dance,
Caught in the universe's trance.
To the edge of time, we take a chance,
Amidst the stars, our hearts advance.

In ethereal light, our dreams reside,
On stardust paths, where we confide.
Eternal whispers, side by side,
In cosmic splendor, we abide.

Timeless echoes gently unfold,
As we explore the stories untold.
Together through the stars of old,
The celestial journey, pure and bold.

Journey to Nowhere

In the silence of forgotten streams,
We wander lost in endless dreams.
Through empty fields and twilight beams,
A journey to nowhere, it seems.

No marked roads or signs in sight,
We roam beneath the ghostly light.
In shadows deep and endless night,
Seeking meaning in our plight.

Through whispering woods and barren land,
We search for truths, our minds command.
In fleeting moments, hand in hand,
The quest unknown, like shifting sand.

No destination, yet we strive,
In every breath, our hope alive.
From dawn till dusk, our hearts derive,
A purpose vast, as we survive.

Wandering through the void's embrace,
We find solace in the space.
In the boundless, unseen place,
A journey to nowhere, we embrace.

Endless Ascent

Upon the peaks of towering height,
We chase the day, and welcome night.
Each step we take, in boundless flight,
An endless ascent, to pure delight.

With skies so vast, and stars so near,
We climb through doubt, and conquer fear.
In the stillness, echoes clear,
To heights unknown, year by year.

Through clouds that whisper dreams anew,
We find the strength to journey through.
In every hue, a timeless view,
Our spirits rise, in skies so blue.

Each summit reached, a new begin,
As heart and soul, the climb within.
In unity, our paths akin,
Eternal ascent, through thick and thin.

Upon the crest, where dreams are spun,
An endless voyage, never done.
Together as one, we face the sun,
In endless ascent, our souls as one.

Heaven's Infinity

Stars that shimmer, night so deep,
Mystery unfolds as silence weeps.
The moon whispers its soft, sweet glow,
In the vastness, truth we seek to know.

Galaxies in their endless dance,
Eternal in their grand expanse.
A canvas painted with divine light,
In Heaven's embrace, day turns to night.

Angels sing in harmonious flight,
Guiding souls to pure delight.
In infinite skies, dreams reside,
Boundless, where love and hope collide.

Heaven's gates of pearly sheen,
Beyond the veil, life's grandest scene.
Eternity calls in tender refrain,
Where joy and peace forever reign.

Seraphim guard with wings alight,
In realms unseen by mortal sight.
Endless horizons, beyond the sphere,
Echoes of grace that all can hear.

The Limitless Reach

Beyond the hills where shadows gleam,
Lies the essence of every dream.
Horizons kissed by the morning hue,
Infinite paths as fresh as dew.

Winds that whisper secrets untold,
Across the plains so free and bold.
Whispering leaves and ocean's drum,
In unity, all things become.

The sun's ascent, a timeless climb,
Marking each moment's fleeting time.
Yet in our hearts, the boundless call,
Reaches beyond the earthly thrall.

Mountains touch the sky's soft veil,
Each summit says, "We will prevail."
In nature's hand, the soul takes flight,
Embracing the eternal height.

In the stretch of every new dawn,
Hope and wonder are reborn.
Each boundary expands our sight,
In the limitless reach of pure delight.

Infinite Vista

Horizon stretches, endless line,
Merging worlds of yours and mine.
Beyond the fields of green and gold,
Lies the stories yet to be told.

Mountains rise with whispers grand,
Guardians of this wondrous land.
Every peak and valley sings,
Of infinite beauty, dreams and wings.

Rivers carve a timeless trace,
In nature's eternal embrace.
Flowing through the sands of life,
Cutting deep with gentle strife.

Skies explode in colors bright,
Chasing darkness, birthing light.
Every dawn, a promise new,
In vibrant shades of azure and blue.

Vast is the canvas, boundless sight,
Unseen realms in gentle flight.
In the infinite vista, we find peace,
Where time and space in union cease.

Cosmic Infinity

Starlight whispers secrets grand,
In the cosmic sea, we understand.
Galaxies twirl in endless grace,
Lost in time and boundless space.

Nebulae weave colors bright,
In the depths of endless night.
From darkness blooms the stars' soft breath,
Crafting life from cosmic death.

Planets dance in silent symphony,
Bound by gravity's solemn decree.
Each orbit writes a tale so old,
In the silence, truth is told.

Comets blaze their transient trail,
Leaving stardust where dreams sail.
Infinite the paths they trace,
Across the universe's face.

Through the night sky's vast array,
Cosmic wonders lead astray.
In the heart of infinity's reach,
We find the truths the stars beseech.

Celestial Brink

On the edge where stars do sing,
A symphony of light they bring,
Their whispers dance in cosmic rings,
At the celestial brink.

Gleaming shards across the sky,
Falling stars say their goodbyes,
A canvas painted bright and high,
A night of sparkling ink.

Galaxies weave in endless tie,
Nebulas in colors vie,
Mysteries in silence lie,
On brink, where dreams they link.

Comets trail with burning breath,
Tracing paths of life and death,
In the vast celestial breadth,
An ethereal sync.

Moons revolve in rhythm's grace,
Casting shadows on Earth's face,
Timeless in their orbital chase,
At the celestial brink.

Unseen Boundaries

Beyond the fields that hearts explore,
Lies the edge of evermore,
With mysteries both calm and sore,
Unseen boundaries soar.

Whispers of the unknown call,
In the quiet, we stand tall,
Where secrets dance and shadows fall,
Through boundaries we implore.

Winds of change in silence sweep,
Over fences buried deep,
In dreams our conscious thoughts we seep,
Beyond the limit's lore.

Paths untaken, roads unseen,
On the fringes of the dream,
Boundaries shifting like a scene,
Of life we know no more.

Whispers of the heart's true aim,
Call us past the borders' frame,
Into realms of nameless name,
Unseen boundaries tame.

Trail of Tomorrow

Paved in hopes and dreams untold,
Steps of courage break the mold,
Onward through the future's fold,
On the trail of tomorrow.

In the dawn, a promise gleams,
Echoes of our silent dreams,
Chasing light through winding streams,
Where the shadows sorrow.

Paths uncharted, brave we stride,
With the stars our only guide,
In the heart where truths reside,
We forge the new to borrow.

Through the mist of upcoming days,
We walk on in endless praise,
Finding strength in new-born ways,
Lighting trails we follow.

Voices of the past may sing,
Yet, it's to the future cling,
With the hope of what we'll bring,
On the trail of tomorrow.

The Constant Path

Through the valleys, over hills,
By the rivers, past the mills,
Guided by the inner thrills,
We walk the constant path.

Seasons change, and winds may blow,
Time moves fast or lingers slow,
Through it all, our hearts will show,
True north within the wraths.

Every step with purpose bound,
In the silence, truth is found,
On this journey firmly ground,
The path of constant faith.

Voices rise and echoes fade,
Through the morning, into shade,
By our choices, paths are laid,
And thus our future craft.

Bound by neither end nor time,
With each step, the mountains climb,
Through the constancy, we chime,
In life's enduring math.

The Unending Journey

Upon the road that twists and bends,
Our footsteps trace where time suspends,
With every mile, new sights unfurl,
A constant quest in this vast world.

Through forests deep and mountains high,
Beneath the stars, across the sky,
The path ahead, unknown yet clear,
With every step, dispelling fear.

The journey's end, a fleeting dream,
Life's river flowing as a stream,
We wander on through night and day,
Forever bound by destiny's sway.

No map can chart the soul's deep quest,
No compass guides the restless breast,
In every heartbeat, every breath,
We find the means to cheat our death.

So onward to horizons wide,
Where mysteries and wonders bide,
The unending journey calls our name,
In endless search, we fan the flame.

Where the Sky Meets Tomorrow

Upon the edge of dawn's first light,
The future lies in shadows bright,
Where morning's promise meets the air,
And hope is born from every prayer.

Beneath the blaze of setting sun,
The day's adventures now are done,
But in the twilight's gentle glow,
Tomorrow's dreams begin to grow.

Through cloudy skies and silver beams,
Life weaves its fabric from our dreams,
We chase the light, we chase the rain,
A dance of joy, a touch of pain.

Where sky and future softly blend,
Unseen horizons have no end,
Each step we take, each breath we breathe,
Shapes the world that we conceive.

In every dawn, in every night,
The boundless echoes of our flight,
Where the sky meets tomorrow's call,
We rise and strive beyond it all.

Ceaseless Day

The morning breaks with golden rays,
Beckoning forth the ceaseless days,
Where time flows like an endless stream,
Awakened by the sun's bright gleam.

From dawn to dusk, life's canvas wide,
In every pulse, in every stride,
We paint with hues both bold and pale,
Each moment tells a living tale.

The hours spin in endless flight,
From morning's blush to quiet night,
Yet time's embrace, we can't contain,
It whispers softly, then remains.

In ceaseless day and silent night,
We seek the truths of inner light,
Unfolding like a lotus bloom,
In timeless dance, we find our room.

So let us revel in the sway,
Of life's profound, ceaseless day,
In every breath, in each heartbeat,
The essence of our being meets.

Wandering Beyond

Into the wild, our spirits roam,
Beyond the fields that we call home,
To places where the heart is free,
In whispered winds and boundless sea.

With every step, a world unfolds,
New stories born, new legends told,
Beneath the sky's expansive dome,
We find a place where dreams can roam.

Through valleys deep and peaks that soar,
Where echoes of adventure roar,
The horizon calls, a siren's song,
In endless quest, we journey on.

Beyond the known, beyond the stars,
We search for life's elusive bars,
In motion, in the endless flight,
We gather essence, day and night.

Let wanderlust our guide remain,
Through joy and sorrow, loss and gain,
For wandering beyond we find,
The deepest truths, in heart and mind.

Journey Without End

Through fields of gold, the path ascends
Where starlight, night and day, extends
Whispers of winds, in chorus blend
Unveiling secrets, skies defend

Each step we take in twilight's hue
Unfurls a world both bright and new
No bounds to dreams that we pursue
An endless tale that life imbues

Mountains rise, then valleys bow
In nature's dance, we make our vow
To seek the answers, here and now
Forevermore, our spirits grow

As rivers flow, so do our minds
In currents strong, our peace we find
A boundless quest, with ties that bind
A journey shared, in fate aligned

From dawn till dusk, the road extends
With every turn, new hope ascends
Our journey's tale is one that bends
Yet never ends, yet never ends

Endless Elysium

In gardens kissed by morning dew
Eternal dreams come into view
A paradise for hearts so true
Where time is but a gentle clue

The flowers bloom in endless spring
With melodies the angels sing
Here joy and love are everything
In every breath, new life they bring

Within the streams, reflections dance
A symphony in pure expanse
Embraced by fate, we take our chance
To weave our souls in love's romance

Beneath the stars, a velvet dome
Where skylines meet, and hearts find home
In endless Elysium, we roam
Forever free, where dreams are sown

Through twilight's hues and dawn's embrace
Our spirits soar in boundless grace
A timeless realm in sacred space
Endless Elysium, our eternal place

Sky Without Borders

Upon the winds of endless blue
No boundaries frame our point of view
Across horizons far and true
The sky without borders calls to you

The sun and moon in cycles fair
Beyond the realms of earth's despair
In freedom found beyond compare
We search for dreams in open air

With wings of hope, we dare to fly
To touch the stars, to kiss the sky
No chains of fear to bind us nigh
Our spirits soar as eagles high

An endless canvas, vast and free
No walls confine our destiny
Amongst the clouds, our hearts decree
To chart the path of mystery

Infinity in every breath
Life's journey vast exceeds our death
In sky without borders, we find our depth
With every flight, we make our step

The Never-ending Pass

Through forests deep and valleys wide
We trek the path where shadows bide
With every turn, new truths we find
A passage carved in hearts and minds

Among the peaks where eagles play
We trace the stars at break of day
With courage drawn from skies of gray
We journey forth, come what may

The winds, our guide, the sun, our fire
In every step, our spirits higher
A tale of old, a new desire
To reach the goals where dreams aspire

Through storms and calm, we tread the way
In darkness, light, both night and day
A timeless pass where life arrays
Its secrets in a grand display

Onward through the endless pass
Where time dissolves like shards of glass
The never-ending path we amass
With every footfall, we surpass

The Evermore Road

Upon the path, where dreams are sown,
A journey vast, through lands unknown,
With every step, the world unfolds,
The Evermore Road, adventure holds.

Beneath the stars, the trail extends,
Where night meets dawn, and shadow blends,
In boundless quest, our spirits roam,
To find the place we call our home.

Through forest deep, and mountains high,
Beyond the reach of mortal eye,
We walk the road, with hearts aglow,
The Evermore, where we must go.

With laughter's echo, tears' embrace,
We mark our trail, our sacred place,
Each footprint tells, a tale untold,
The Evermore, an endless gold.

So on we tread, through time and space,
To find our truth, our destined grace,
Forevermore, the road shall be,
A path to endless liberty.

Boundless Bosom

In the arms of Earth, we find our rest,
On boundless bosom, cradled best,
Through seasons' change, and life's stern test,
The heart of nature, gives its nest.

With gentle breeze, and rustling leaves,
The boundless bosom, life receives,
From dawn's first light, to twilight's eve,
In nature's lap, we find reprieve.

The rivers course, through valleys green,
A boundless grace, in every scene,
The oceans vast, the skies serene,
Nature's love, a bond unseen.

The flowers bloom, in colors wild,
In boundless bosom, tender, mild,
We walk the world, as nature's child,
In her embrace, forever styled.

With every heartbeat, earth and man,
In boundless bosom, life's great plan,
Together weave, since time began,
The sacred bond, 'twixt earth and man.

Endless Ascendancy

From humble earth, to heights unknown,
We rise forever, spirit-grown,
In endless quest, through realms unshown,
To claim the stars, as seeds are sown.

With every climb, the sky aligns,
An endless path, where sunray shines,
Through trials hard, and sacred signs,
We seek the peak, where soul defines.

Above the clouds, where eagles fly,
Endless ascendancy, we try,
To reach the summit, touch the sky,
With hearts on fire, dreams drawn nigh.

In every step, through faith and fear,
The mountain's call, forever near,
We conquer heights, with vision clear,
And carve our names, in skies austere.

As long as stars in heaven gleam,
Endless ascendancy, our theme,
We chase the light, and live the dream,
To rise above, in endless stream.

Infinite Beyond

Beyond the veil of mortal sight,
Lies the realm of endless night,
Where dreams take flight, on wings of light,
The infinite beyond, our guiding might.

In the cosmos vast, we find our place,
In endless dance, through time and space,
With stars as guides, in this embrace,
We journey forth, to worlds apace.

Through nebulae, and astral seas,
We sail the winds of cosmic breeze,
Infinite beyond, with endless ease,
Our spirits soar, and find their keys.

With every star, a tale unfolds,
Of cosmic truths, and mysteries old,
In infinite beyond, our hearts behold,
The secrets of the universe told.

In twilight's glow, and dawn's first beam,
We chase the light, beyond the dream,
To infinite beyond, where wonders teem,
Our souls alight, in cosmic gleam.

The Never-Ending Line

In twilight's gentle sway, a tale unfolds,
The canvas wide, with colors bold,
A journey starts, no end defined,
A path that's drawn, with heart aligned.

Through fields of gold, and silver streams,
A thread of hope, in woven dreams,
Wanderlust, a guiding star,
To lands unknown, both near and far.

Mountains high, and valleys low,
Eternal road, where breezes blow,
Step by step, in rhythm's rhyme,
Onward bound, with endless time.

Whispers of the twilight chill,
Echoes carried, soft and still,
In lines of fate, entwined and fine,
We walk the never-ending line.

Horizons stretch, to realms unseen,
In every note, and shade of green,
Life's design, a masterpiece divine,
Forever drawn, the never-ending line.

Above and Beyond

Skies that whisper tales of yore,
And dreams that soar forevermore,
A realm where shadows cease to be,
Above the clouds, we wander free.

With wings of light, and hearts of gold,
To unknown heights, our stories told,
Beyond the stars, through cosmic flight,
We chase the dawn, the endless night.

Mirrors of the sunlit gleam,
Reflections in a boundless stream,
Infinite the paths we tread,
Above and beyond, where hearts are led.

Celestial waves, the ocean's crest,
A universe, our boundless quest,
Horizons merge, the sky and sea,
A journey grand, for you and me.

Through cosmic dance, the galaxies spin,
In vast expanse, where dreams begin,
We sail on winds, both fierce and kind,
Above and beyond, our souls unbind.

Heartbeat of the Cosmos

In the silence of the night,
Stars disclose their ancient light,
Whispers from the void immense,
Heartbeat of the vast expanse.

Galaxies in spiraled grace,
Spread their wings in boundless space,
Echoes from the time unknown,
Resonating, star dust grown.

Nebulas with colors bright,
Paint the skies with hues of light,
A symphony, so rich, so grand,
Cosmic rhymes at our command.

Planets spin in cosmic dance,
Orbits drawn in sheer expanse,
Rhythms set by unseen hands,
In cadence with the cosmic bands.

The universe, a living stream,
Pulses with an endless dream,
Listen to its silent beat,
In every star, in every fleet.

Trace of Infinity

In every grain of sand, a story lies,
A trace of time, beneath our eyes,
Infinite the worlds within,
A universe where dreams begin.

Leaves that fall in autumn's breath,
Whisper secrets, life and death,
Cycles turn, eternity,
In every leaf, infinity.

River's flow, the oceans wide,
Flowing through the years untied,
Boundless as the stars that gleam,
Each drop partakes the endless stream.

Mountains rise and valleys dip,
Echoes through the ages slip,
Silent keepers of the lore,
Trace of time forevermore.

In our hearts, a spark divine,
Mirrors of the grand design,
Life's a canvas, wide and free,
Painted with infinity.

Ephemeral Edge

A fleeting glance, a whispered cry
Under twilight's amber dome
Moments dance, and then they fly
Beyond the realm we call our home

Petals fall from summer's bloom
Landing soft on morning dew
In this world, the slightest gloom
Softly fades from vivid view

Shadowed corners, light we chase
Bound by time's relentless thread
Waves of life, an endless race
Toward the line where hearts are fed

In the quiet, secrets drift
Echoes of a vanished song
Through the veil, where colors lift
A tapestry where dreams belong

So we stand on fragile ground
Breathing in the day's soft pledge
In each moment, we are found
Ever near the ephemeral edge

Unfurling Sky

Open wide the canvas high
Palette born of sun and mist
Brushstrokes in the morning sky
Heaven's colors deftly kissed

Whispers of the wind's embrace
Carry tales of distant seas
Clouds that dance in feathered grace
Woven with the autumn breeze

Stars will soon adorn the night
Gleaming in their silent choir
Launching dreams to endless flight
Phantoms lit by silver fire

Dawn will break with hues anew
Blazing trails where shadows lie
Every morn, a newborn view
Wonders in the unfurling sky

Gaze upon the boundless height
Find within the heart's true aim
Through each day and each new night
Endless skies remain the same

Uncharted Expanse

Where the maps have yet to tread
Through the fog of mystery
Paths unknown are softly spread
In the land of history

Footsteps find the virgin ground
Laden with the dew of night
Echoes of a distant sound
Calling hearts to newfound light

Beyond the reach of tethered fate
Horizons open wide and bare
Destiny will never wait
For those who seek, for those who dare

Mountains, valleys, oceans deep
Guarded by the ancient lore
In their silent watch they keep
Secrets on a far-flung shore

So we journey, bold and free
Guided by a silent trance
Leading us to what will be
In the vast, uncharted expanse

Boundless Trail

Through the fields where rivers flow
Underneath the shadowed trees
Paths untamed by time's soft blow
Whispers ride upon the breeze

Footprints mark the dusty way
Silent echoes of the past
In this realm where moments sway
Boundless dreams are ever cast

Stars align to guide us forth
Night's embrace, our beacon bright
Journeying from south to north
Held within the heart's own light

Every turn and every bend
Holds a tale, a secret wail
Winding roads that never end
Woven in the boundless trail

We, adventurers of time
Craft the stories, blaze the way
Travel on, to heights we climb
In the song of night and day

The Limitless Ascend

Beneath the stars' eternal gaze,
Horizons stretch to far-off days,
Mountains whisper ancient songs,
In valleys, whispers play along.

Climbing peaks with fearless stride,
Above the clouds where eagles glide,
Steps to realms where dreams reside,
On paths where hopes and hearts abide.

Through mists and shadows, pure and bright,
Destiny's call, a guiding light,
Ascending high, no end in sight,
In boundless skies, our spirit's flight.

Faraway Dreams

In twilight's hush, where whispers meet,
Lies a world both soft and sweet,
Rivers of silver, skies that gleam,
Within the realm of faraway dreams.

Through fields of stars and moonlit dew,
Minds drift away to lands anew,
Castles of hope, in silken seams,
Woven in night, faraway dreams.

Mountains of wonders, seas of calm,
In this land of endless charm,
Boundless skies and endless streams,
Journey on through faraway dreams.

Perennial Route

Through woodland paths, both wild and free,
Where roots entwine and ancient trees,
The perennial route unfolds its way,
A timeless journey, day by day.

Whispers of the forest, in the breeze,
Tell of legends, old decrees,
Rivers carve their ageless path,
In nature's prose, the aftermath.

Seasons change, yet ever still,
The route unfurls, with nature's will,
A symphony of time and truth,
Everlasting, perennial route.

Always Ahead

Steps in sync with heartbeats' thrum,
Chasing shadows, on journeys begun,
Eyes set forward, never to tread,
On paths behind, but always ahead.

Mountains call with peaks of gold,
Stories of daring yet untold,
A horizon where the sun has fled,
Guides our dreams, always ahead.

Stars ignite in the darkened sky,
Future's promise, a burning high,
With every dawn, new paths are spread,
Eternal quest, always ahead.

Eternity's Edge

On the precipice of time, we stand
Worlds unfold in our open hands
Moments cascade like rivers wide
Boundless tides we cannot hide

Whispers of fate on the wind's soft voice
Drawing us near without a choice
Into the starlit expanse we leap
In secrets of night, our dreams we keep

Veils of dusk around us spin
Promises of what's never been
Gazing into night's deep abyss
We find our solace, we reminisce

Through endless shadows, paths unseen
Mysteries linger where we've been
Yet forward on this edge we tread
Eternal bound, forever led

Celestial Continuum

Stars align in cosmic rhyme
Through the vast expanse of time
Galaxies spiral, weaving light
Ephemeral dance of day and night

Dim echoes hum of lives long past
In whispers of a universe so vast
Planets waltz in silent grace
Bridging the heavens' endless space

In twilight's glow, the nebulae bloom
Creation's spark dispels the gloom
Constellations mark our lore
Eternal tales forevermore

Through dark expanse and radiant glow
The cosmic currents ebb and flow
In the continuum, we find our place
A fleeting glimpse in time's embrace

Infinite Embrace

In the boundless twilight's hue
Endless skies of somber blue
Within the stars, our hearts entwine
Lost in realms both yours and mine

Silent whispers, shadows deep
In dreams' embrace, our souls do seep
Traversing nights of endless grace
Infinity within this space

Boundless love, no time, no end
Eternal flame, our hearts transcend
As the galaxies collide
In this vast expanse, we hide

In the fold of time's embrace
Moments linger, soft and chaste
In endless firmament, we float
On waves of love, our heartbeats wrote

Perpetual Distance

Across the void, our gazes meet
Silent echoes, bittersweet
Bound by ties we cannot see
In distant realms, we're meant to be

Through time and space, a silent plea
For closeness in our galaxy
Wistful dreams, the nights extend
Love's beacon shines, we won't pretend

In the shadows, we exist
Yearning hearts in starlit mist
Infinite miles our fates divide
Yet forever, you reside inside

Endless threads of time we chase
Within the stars, we find our place
Though the distance may persist
In each heartbeat, we resist

Infinite Twilight

In the dusk's embrace, stars softly gleam,
Whispers of night caress the stream.
Shadows dance with a mystic grace,
In twilight's arms, I find my place.

Moon's gentle light spills on the earth,
Silent echoes of day's rebirth.
Dreams awaken in twilight's glow,
Secrets of night, gently bestow.

Lanterns of sky blink, soft and faint,
In the twilight, stars paint.
A canvas vast, of deepest hue,
In twilight's heart, dreams renew.

Nightingales sing a song pure,
In twilight's hush, hearts endure.
Whispers of winds through leaves so light,
Infinite twilight, purest delight.

As night deepens, stars break free,
Boundless twilight, eternity.
In the silence, dreams take flight,
Infinite realms of endless night.

Unbound Horizons

Beyond the hills where skies expand,
Horizons stretch, uncharted land.
In the whisper of the dawn,
A new horizon, ever drawn.

Eyes set on the distant line,
Future paths and dreams entwine.
Boundless skies, azure sea,
Horizons call, to be free.

Mountains high and valleys deep,
Dreams and hopes in currents sweep.
Unbound horizons, endless quest,
In the unknown, find our best.

Sunrise paints horizons bold,
Stories of life all untold.
Infinite paths under the sky,
Horizons beckon, spread wings and fly.

In the distance, truths unfold,
Horizons vast, dreams take hold.
Limitless skies and boundless seas,
Unbound horizons, spirit frees.

Journey's Infinite Splendor

With each step, paths intertwine,
Journeys of heart, soul's design.
Endless roads, dreams ascend,
In journey's splendor, stories blend.

Mountains call with echoing voice,
Paths unknown; a daring choice.
Footsteps on the ancient ground,
Journey's splendor, profound.

Whispering winds and roaring seas,
Journey's call, spirit frees.
In every breath, every mile,
Journey's splendor, embrace the trial.

Stars above, and earth below,
Journey's light begins to glow.
By day we seek, by night we find,
Journey's splendor, hearts aligned.

Endless quests, dreams to render,
Journey's infinite, boundless splendor.
In each horizon, new wonders lie,
Journey's splendor, reaching the sky.

The Unmeasured Path

In the shadow of ancient trees,
Unmeasured path winds and weaves.
Steps unknown, heart's desire,
On this path, spirits conspire.

Through the wild, untamed, free,
Path unmeasured, destiny.
Every twist, a story untold,
Path of wonders, brave and bold.

In the silence, whispers clear,
Path unmeasured, devoid of fear.
Journey onward, light or dark,
Unmeasured path, eternal spark.

Crossing rivers, climbing heights,
Path unmeasured, pure delights.
In each moment, breath anew,
Unmeasured path, spirit's view.

Endless journey, boundless scope,
Unmeasured path, heart's hope.
From dawn to dusk, across the land,
Unmeasured path, firmly stand.

The Infinite Divide

Between the stars, a line unseen
A chasm vast, a void serene
Yet whispers faint on twilight's crest
Echo the dreams of hearts unblessed

Each star, a beacon, silent and bright
Guides the lost through endless night
Ancient stories in constellations found
Of love and sorrow, profound, unbound

Through cosmic seas, our spirits glide
Bound by the pull of the infinite tide
In silence, we find a wordless guide
To navigate the infinite divide

Lost in the dance of celestial fire
We gaze beyond, forever higher
Yearning hearts in starlit strands
Formed by cosmic, divine hands

Time and space in tandem twine
A delicate thread, both yours and mine
Together in eternity's stride
Bound forever by the infinite divide

Limitless Pathways

Wanderers on paths unknown
With dreams and hopes, not alone
Each step a whisper, courage calls
Through shadows deep, as silence falls

Mountains high and valleys low
Through forests dense and rivers' flow
The journey, vast, the soul's embrace
Unfolding tales in endless space

Footprints fade in sands of time
Beyond horizons, we climb
Limitless pathways to explore
Seeking always, yearning more

Guided by the heart's true north
We venture forth, undeterred, henceforth
In boundless realms, our spirits spry
To touch the earth, to touch the sky

In our hearts, a compass lies
To traverse where eternity defies
Together, we'll find our way
Through the limitless pathways, come what may

The Unending Chase

In fields of gold, beneath the sky
We chase the sun as days go by
A quest for dreams that never cease
An unending chase, hearts never lease

Through morn's soft light, we run in haste
In twilight's glow, no time to waste
Each moment fleeting, yet we try
To grasp the stars, to learn to fly

With every step, our spirits soar
Through unknown realms, to distant shores
An endless journey, bound by grace
A timeless race, the unending chase

Through storms fierce and gentle breeze
We gather strength with each heartbeat's seize
For in pursuit, we find our place
In the dance of the unending chase

From dawn to dusk, under moon's soft gaze
We navigate through cosmic maze
With hearts ablaze, in endless space
We embrace the eternal, unending chase

The Eternal Loop

In cycles old, forever bound
A journey infinite, profound
Through time's embrace, the loop begins
Echoes of past with future twins

Steps retraced on paths worn thin
An endless dance, where we begin
Each moment new, yet strangely known
In rings of time, eternally sown

As moonlight fades and sun does rise
We wander through familiar skies
Caught in patterns, life begets
Twined in threads, no soul forgets

Through endless loops, our hearts entwine
In fate's embrace, a grand design
Both old and new, in constant swoop
We voyage through the eternal loop

Yearning for the end and start
In circles bound, yet far apart
In every loop, our spirits bloom
Within the endless, the eternal loop